BHARAT
Vishwa Guru that was before Invasion

SHYAM SINGH

BLUEROSE PUBLISHERS
India | U.K.

Copyright © Shyam Singh 2024

All rights reserved by author. No part of this publication may be reproduced, stored in a retrieval system or transmitted in any form or by any means, electronic, mechanical, photocopying, recording or otherwise, without the prior permission of the author. Although every precaution has been taken to verify the accuracy of the information contained herein, the publisher assumes no responsibility for any errors or omissions. No liability is assumed for damages that may result from the use of information contained within.

BlueRose Publishers takes no responsibility for any damages, losses, or liabilities that may arise from the use or misuse of the information, products, or services provided in this publication.

For permissions requests or inquiries regarding this publication, please contact:

BLUEROSE PUBLISHERS
www.BlueRoseONE.com
info@bluerosepublishers.com
+91 8882 898 898
+4407342408967

ISBN: 978-93-6452-120-8

Cover Design: Sadhna Kumari
Typesetting: Pooja Sharma

First Edition: August 2024

I, Sewak Shyam Singh surrender everything in the lotus feet of Vibhuti. Whatever I am writing here I am writing it by the blessing and permission of Vidhata. By the will of the supreme divine, I am writing this book for the protection of the people who are the descendants of Bharat Mata.

I will forever be grateful for everything my mother has done for me. She is the reason for every good that I ever had and ever will have. Due to her blessing I know about anything divine in nature.

This book is the first book of the series of books which will have all the truth and strategies that can help the people of Akhand Bharat at any point of time to strengthen themselves, protect themselves and know their true potential.

Before you begin to read keep this in mind many sentences have their own hidden meanings and messages which if found will help you a lot. So, kindly try to be a learning adventurer first, to hunt the treasure of great wisdom that can lead you to the strongest weapon that there is today and hidden well in plain sight only to be found by the worthy who bears the strength to wield it.

Contents

Chapter 1: Intellectual barrier to be broken first............ 1

Chapter 2: Akhand Bharat A Vishwa Guru That Was...5

Chapter 3: Dharma is the only right path to walk on.. 8

Chapter 4: Akhand Bharat the supreme and beautiful creation.. 13

Chapter 5: The beginning of invasion in Akhand Bharat.. 18

Chapter 6: The invasion to destroy us, that has not stopped yet.. 22

CHAPTER 1

Intellectual barrier to be broken first...

To think of Bharat as a Vishwa Guru again, might look to you as a dream but it is the everlasting essence of the true Sanatan Sanskriti (eternal culture) of the Akhand Bharat.

The country which we live in today is only Bharat, not the actual Akhand Bharat. To become the Akhand Bharat again is to be the actual Bharat again not only as a country but also as a rastra, as an individual, as a family, as a society and as a national diversified yet united idea.

A country is not just only a piece of land on the map of the world, it is also a union of people who know, feel and believe that the piece of land from which they come is their motherland. A rashtra is of the people who have their own culture and civilisational ideology to live with in their motherland. So a country is a land, its people and their cultural ideology through which they uniquely identify themselves with.

Today's India, thinks of itself to be only a country to exist after 1947; which is the real intellectual barrier for today's Indians to not completely accept themself as one so mighty to have the strength to rule all over the world and which always chooses to still be so immensely strong yet be at peace to not wage a war first. By intellectual barrier, what I mean is you are limiting your true strength of being an Indian in your own intellect by not imagining right, by not thinking right, by not learning right and by not believing right about your own country.

Your inability to think that your culture is not great, your history is not great, your ancestors were not great, your scriptures are not great becomes the reason for your low self esteem to ultimately make you less worthy of anything good that there is and which you might have deserved. The main reason for our weakness is our disbelief, to think that we need somebody else to depend upon for our source of strength. Historically we always were the strongest warriors, the mightiest rulers, the greatest culture, the smartest civilisation, the blessed people of god, the powerful kingdom, the prosperous society.

We the descendants of the legendary people of Akhand Bharat have always been like Shri Ramdoot Hanuman ji, who are one of the strongest warriors of the Shri Ram sena yet today are unable to know our true strength due to a curse. The curse is the inability to believe, accept and trust our own truth as a reality, which could help us to boost our self confidence. This curse is simple and can easily be uplifted just like Jamvant ji did for Hanuman ji. We will have to ultimately believe in our responsible decision making ability with reason, logic, proof and facts. Then only we will become the strongest civilians of the land of Bharat.

To be Bharat rastra is to be a country, a culture, a civilisation which exists from the beginning of any of the recorded history of intellectual society of today from anywhere in the world. And by being that to have the mindset of a sage who existed so long and lived enough to know it all yet be an invincible warrior to protect it all.

Bharat a Vishwa Guru does not only have the responsibility to become strong militarily, economically, administratively and culturally. It is its right, like the actual Sampurna Swarajya and should be the sole purpose to become great with its education, finances, individual strength (all five: intellectual, physical, emotional, financial and social strengths) and moral as well as idealistic beliefs.

The responsibility for the growth of Bharat, the rashtra, is not only of the administration and governments, the responsibility for protection of the land of Bharat is not only of the military and armed forces, the responsibility to educate all is not only of the educational institutions and teachers, the responsibility to create jobs for people to be employed is not only of the companies and state; all these necessary responsibilities are also the responsibilities of every individual who is the child of the motherland maa Bharti. Every individual of the Bharat rastra has a responsibility to fulfill by just being born in it, that with every step they take, every decision they make, they are to contribute through their dharma, kriya, karma and karmafal only for the the betterment and increase in strength of the matrubhumi that is the motherland maa Bharti.

Bharat mata is mata of the descendents of the Sanatan sanskriti the Bhartiyas that is the Hindus, the Sikh, the

Sindhis, the Jains, the Buddhists and the believers of devta and devi of any part of the land. Bharat mata is also the mata, the mother of all who live in this punya bhumi and are united by being the children of Bharat, the one who all are now the Bhartiyas are also the Parsis, the Jews, the Muslims, the Christians and all the ones whose ancestors belonged to this matrubhumi. Due to this belonging, this being born on the sacred motherland, it is now not only the responsibility and the rightful duty of all children of Bharat mata be it hindus, sikhs, buddhists, jains, sindhis, parsis, jews, muslims, christians and the children of this land to protect, preserve, liberate, strengthen, takecare, educate, maintain and rescue everything of this rastra; the history, culture, heritage, techniques, flora and fauna, forest, animal, land, food, knowledge, wisdom, wealth, ideas, people, rivers and everything that belongs to this greater than heaven motherland by becoming one of many and yet being one with many.

Where one is born the place becomes their motherland and it is their rightful duty to protect everything of the motherland as they would have protected what was of their mother. As a mother is always the closest to the children, so is the motherland always superior and closest to the person born on that land not only due to their birth on the land but also due to the culture, the nourishment, the education and many more different factors they get and should always be grateful about.

The mother and the motherland is always superior to anyone be it god himself and anything be it gold itself.

janani janmabhoomischa swargadapi gariyasi

Chapter 2

Akhand Bharat
A Vishwa Guru That Was...

The Bharat Rastra which lived in the ancient civilisation was the solution and the answer of all the problems and the questions that ever existed in the whole world at any point of time. As the divine soul has all the answers to all the questions of mind and knows the truth about one's reason for the existence of being a human, so was the Akhand Bharat. Bharat was the awakened consciousness of the ancient world which had all the spiritual wisdom, ancient scriptures and cultural heritage to not only benefit its own people but also the world they lived with. But the disaster of invasion came due to which wealth in the form of treasure, wisdom in the form of scriptures and strength in the form of protectors all got destroyed within thousands of years.

It is not that the ancient times were great or the world was great, it was the people of Bharat that made the world a better place to live, through their wisdom, techniques, teachings and perspective to see the world as "Vasudhaiva Kutumbakam" meaning "The world is one family". Through this realization that every being that exists is alive only by the will of Param Brahma himself the supreme creator of all existence and life.

The scholars, the sages, the rishis, the gurus, the kings, the queens the philosophers, the munis, the gyanis, the tapasvis and rest of the highly intellectual bhartiyas (all the people of Akhand Bharat) viewed the living beings .i.e all humans, animals, mountains, waterbodies, reptiles, plants, land, etc., only as children of Dharti mata (mother Earth) and treated them equally as they would treat one of their own to live with them in harmony. As our ancestors they had the responsibility to liberate the world through their truthful wisdom they also had the responsibility to strengthen their own. To make themself strong our ancestors had four principles to follow that were first the Dharma, second the Aartha, third the Kama and fourth also most important of all the Moksha. As the four pillars of strength existed, four pillars of one's own weakness were also kept in check to never be accepted, as being first the Kama (lust), second the Krodh (anger), third the Lobh (greed) and fourth also the worst of all the Moh (attachment).

In the ancient Sanatan Sanskriti the most important and strongest individual position to hold was of a guru rather than of the king himself. Ultimately the guru could be any one who was a sadhu, a rishi, a maharishi, a brahmrishi, a yogi, a tapasvi, an acharya cause all these people had one thing in common which was being so intellectually profound as a person to be called an expert in their own field. Every field that there was, is today, or will ever exist in the future from warfare to harmony, union to one, individual to none, stranger to king, art to destruction, beggar to being, idiot to genius, eternal elixir to poison for kill and etc. A guru holded so much power in that day society not only because of their abundant knowledge but also for their greatest regard to help all by being kind to all and treat all as equal. All these gurus used to unify all the kingdoms of kings and queens by creating many equally benefitting relations and bilateral agreements among parties due to which they played a very important role for the ancient Akhand Bharat to make it strong militarily, economically, culturally, administratively, and socially. In the sovereign, socialist, secular, democratic, republic of today's Bharat, when people choose a leader they choose them only for their intellectual strength that helps the people to believe in their vision. So the gurus of the ancient Akhand Bharat were intellectually strong-minded, straight forward, sheer willed, rational, reasonable, down-to-earth, hyper focused individuals and more important of all they were idealistic visionaries. As they say "be careful of what you are trying to be, cause to be is to become". So, the Akhand Bharat, in itself was a guru and that's why when the world came for answers of its questions they realized the land was the teacher to the world. As the moon is there in the night to save us from complete darkness, so were the gurus to save human civilization from the darkness of ignorance and desires.

अज्ञानतिमिरान्धस्य ज्ञानाञ्जनशालाकया ।

चक्षुरुन्मीलितं येन तस्मै श्रीगुरवे नमः ॥

Agyan timir-andhasya Gyananjan Shalakaya.

Chakshur-oonmeelitam yena tasmai Shri Gurave Namah.

My Salutations to that reverent Guru, who opened my inner eyes and removed the darkness of ignorance from my blind eyes by applying the light of self-knowledge.

Chapter 3

Dharma is the only right path to walk on......

The ancient Vishwa guru Akhand Bharat knew that Dharma is the only right path to walk on. Which brings a deeper sense of awareness about the responsibilities to all of our actions as a choice for surrendering to Atman known as the divine soul. Dharma is the righteous conduct of one in such a way that all dutiful actions are performed with nonattachment to become selfless service of paramatman and those dutiful actions taken then become the param dharma which becomes the reason for one's attainment of moksha to the ParamDhaam.

"Dharmo Rakshati Rakshitah " means you protect dharma, and dharma shall protect you. It can be understood with an example like a mother being dutiful towards her child taking care of everything as education, food, sanitation, wellness, listening to the child, being his friend, a great parent,etc but more importantly teaching him or her about their duties and responsibilities also about what is right and what is wrong, creating a deep understanding of righteous judgment within him or her due to which when the child becomes a man or a woman in the future they take care of their mother, father, family, children, household, society and nation. By this now we understand why the gurus were doing what they were doing. When the prince or the princess is taught about their rightful duties towards the kingdom and their people by the gurus, they become great king and queen due to which the kingdom becomes great, people are treated well, peasants are educated truthfully and protected well and the businesses in the kingdom run swiftly by proper conduct towards them with law and order. This is what had happened in the past, the recent example being the duo of guru and shishya which is the duo of the great guru Vishnu gupta also known as Chanakya and the shishya Chandragupta Maurya. Acharya Chanakya was fed up with the Nanda dynasty's unrighteous actions and adharma in the Patliputra today's Patna due to which he selected an ideal candidate a child named Chandragupta Maurya who later on became the new king in the Patliputra due to his guidance. Acharya taught Maurya everything he knew about like warfare, politics, economics, strategic relations, astrology, psychology, medicine, poison, etc., to shape him into being a capable leader with humility and excellence in governance for the kingdom and people of his kingdom.

As is said by the wise; the strong can never be destroyed by the unrelated, they can only be perished by the betrayal of their own; let them be the king by his ministers, leader by their followers. So did our own were the first reason of our destruction who didn't follow the path of dharma due to their deep attachments towards their desires and them being in the position of king, ministers of the king, senapati (commander-in-chief), or other positions that holded strong social significance with money, power, fame or knowledge in the then society. Those arrogant idiots being fond of themselves in their own mind and then betraying their dharma of protecting the culture, the land, the people and the knowledge led down to the destruction of our greater than heaven mathrubhumi maa Bharti and its beautiful Sanatan Sanskriti. Let them be the asuras Hiranyaksha or Hiranyakashipu, Ravana or Kumbhkaran, the asur buddhis Sishupala or Duryodhana, the Kali Purusa or the people of kalyug with unrighteous conduct toward others. People of this kind of mindset will always be the reason for the destruction of their own country, culture and civilization due to their wrongful conduct with whatever they get their hands upon.

The ten heads of Ravana represented many things of dharma till he was a dharmi purus (righteous man) but when he became the adharmi purus (unrighteous man). Those ten heads became the representation of ten qualities which can lead any human being to their own destruction and demise. Those ten qualities were kama (lust), krodha (anger), lobha (greed), moha (delusion), mada (pride), maatsarya (envy), buddhi (intellect), manas (mind), chitta (will), and ahamkara (ego).

One who surrenders to their own attachments rather than their duties of existence shall have all the pain, suffering, sorrow and misery as the punishments to betray their kartavya dharma. This is the word of the supreme divine trinity, the Tridevs and the Tridevis. The tridev are union of Parampujya Shri Pita Bramha father of creation and life, Prabhu Shri Hari Vishnu preserver of all creation and harmony of life, and Rudradev Guru Shiv destroyer and sangharak of creation when the time ends. Same as the Tridevs, the Tridevis are the union of Mata MahaSaraswati, mother of all knowledge and wisdom, Mata MahaLakshmi, mother of all wealth and prosperity and Mata Jagatbhagwati Parvati, mother of power and energy.

As there are ten qualities for the destruction of a being there are also ten qualities for the upliftment, development and enlightenment of the being. These ten qualities are also the pillars and rules of dharma which are Dhriti (patience), kshama (forgiveness), dama (self-control), asteya (honesty), sauch (sanctity), indriya-nigraha (control of all senses), dhi (benevolent intellect and reason), vidya (knowledge and learning), satya (truthfulness), and akrodha (absence of anger).One who surrenders to dharma for fulfilling their duties of existence and detaches themselves from their desires shall have peace, prosperity, joy and freedom as a reward for being loyal to their kartavya karma. This is also the word of supreme divine Trimurti.

श्रेयान्स्वधर्मो विगुण: परधर्मात्स्वनुष्ठितात् । स्वभावनियतं कर्म कुर्वन्नाप्नोति किल्बिषम् ॥

Shreyān swa-dharmo viguṇaḥ para-dharmāt sv-anuṣhṭhitāt

svabhāva-niyatam karma kurvan nāpnoti kilbiṣham

It is better to do one's own dharma, even though imperfectly, than to do another's dharma, even though perfectly. By doing one's innate duties, a person does not incur sin.

अच्छी प्रकार आचरण किये हुए दूसरे के धर्म से गुण रहित भी अपना धर्म श्रेष्ठ है, क्योंकि स्वभाव से नियत किये हुए स्वधर्म रूप कर्म को करता हुआ मनुष्य पाप को नहीं प्राप्त होता

Chapter 4

Akhand Bharat the supreme and beautiful creation...

As a country grows to become immensely strong and if the ego of that strength takes over the heads of the country's leadership they start to think of their dominance over others in the world. World dominance has always been there since human existence started to have desires and that will exist till humans start to completely control their desires. Few examples from the recent past of world dominance through invasion are: World War 1, World War 2, Pakistan in parts of India's Kashmir, Chinese invasion in today's Tibet, Hong Kong, East Turkestan, Taiwan, parts of India's Ladakh region called Aksai Chin and others countries. Countries with the vision of world dominance can't see the greater real picture, that you can invade a strong or not so strong country but can't control it no matter what and can't have it for too long no matter what. Few examples from the recent past are: the Invasion of Britain, French and Portuguese in many other countries to make them their colonies including Bharat. Today the reason for international conflict of borders between countries is many times idiotic but the ultimate goal is to have the land and resources of others for their own. In many parts of the world, the form of governance in the country for the people and land is just a joke. If the form of governance in a country will just be only for its people then the land's resources like rivers, minerals, forests, animals, birds, etc and the culture of the land will ultimately be used for their destruction to benefit its people in monetary value and unnecessary comfort in the name of unreasonable development. Any form of governance in the country should not only be for the people but also for the land and the culture of the land equally chosen by the people with sustainable form of development. For people to have their own unique identity, it is necessary for them to be identified through their own culture of their ancestors and the land they have today, which will always have to be protected by them at all cost.

Many countries think of themselves and their culture to be better than others due to which they dive deep with their attachments towards their belief and forgetting what the actual lessons of their culture meant. Any culture, literature, technique or wisdom that ever existed from the beginning of the first intellectually reasonable humans, only existed for the upliftment of human society and the individual's consciousness to be enlightened for their own awakening. This was because when humans become one with the cosmic divine powers through their awakened consciousness, they get to relate with the creation and the divine which helps them to be free of their worries of tomorrow, their attachment with pain of their past and let them be able to live a peaceful today in harmony with themselves and others.

Out of all the creations which are created by the supreme divine, there are only three which have the quality and capability to relate and connect with everything that there is in the created existence and those three are firstly the supreme creation itself, second the prakriti or mother nature and third the humans who are the children of the supreme creation and the priktiti.

The true meaning of strength is to let things be as what they are supposed to be according to dharma and become the protector of the righteousness to be finally free from all the attachments, so that one's own divinity can be experienced and utilized to put into service for the greater good. But this is the only thing the world tends to forget every time and that's why Bharat always becomes the center of attention for the whole world either being a supremely advanced civilisation with technology or the center of wealth and wisdom, or the center of art and heritage or the center of politics and power or the center of yoga and spirituality. In one way or another, in one era or the other, Bharat was, is and always will be the only country to have the means to achieve whatever one desires to have. Bharat as a land is itself divine, as culture is itself supreme, as a person is itself karmayogi because it is the only land on the whole Earth for which the rest was created by the will of Vidhata. Bharat is the supreme and beautiful creation of the Vibhuti because without a mind body cannot move so the world without Bharat will be unable to know life or to live the life it deserves. The rastra teaches how to be a human, what it is to be a human, why to be a good human and for whom to be the righteous human. Everything comes down to just being selfless and to be a sewak, who performs the necessary rights and duties for all the responsibility one has, as a form of service towards the divine. Bharat is the only land where a king leaves everything he has to uplift and liberate the civilisation like the ancient civil engineer and hydrologist Suryavanshi Maharaja Bhagirath did. He was the one true and rightful king of his time who performed his duties towards his people and brought the river goddess Mata Ganga from heaven to this great Bharatbhumi.

Bharat is the only land where every human, no matter male or female, has necessarily 16 sanskars to perform regardless of their position in the society from coming into the womb to leaving the body after their death to reach the paramdhaam and to be ultimately liberated from the continuous cycle of life and death.

Bharat is the only civilisation that says not to be greedy for the heaven's throne nor to be worried about hell's punishment from sins one committed when performing one's own duty only to attain mukti.

Enlightenment is not the question of facts and figures, but it is the question of one's own way to experience it through complete surrender and sheer belief in the wisdom of the shakti of sanatan. Bharat before being a country is a land of the divine where the supreme creator themselves take avatar in many different forms to destroy adharma, adharmai, their followers and unrighteousness; then strengthen dharma, dharmis, their descendants and righteousness to make people follow their path for one's own upliftment to parmarth through shiksha, sanskars, sanskriti and parampara. Bharat the land is to be protected by the people born in it, lived in it, or taken saran in it because it is the most beautiful creation of the supreme divine itself, otherwise one will be punished with no empathy for their sin in hell, for entire eternity committed against the dharma of the land, of the rastra, of the ancestors, of the civilisation and of the divine's will.

Bharat the land which firstly protects, secondly preserves, thirdly strengthens, fourthly uplifts and lastly elevates anyone or anything in it's boundary through all its resources, wisdom, way of worship and many other factors but most important of all grants freedom to every individual in many tangible and intangible ways. Bharat is also the most beautiful and supreme land as a creation of the divine because it is the gateway which leads to the paradise of the divine which is a place where pure souls who performed param dharma belong called the Muktidham. Muktidham has many definitions but one to be particularly focus upon is, Muktidham is a paradise above, greater and powerful than hell and heaven, where one will be in the presence on the divine and from where no one will be sent back to misery of continuous cycle of life and death, also where the pure souls will become one with the Param Brahma and connect with the truth of creation and existence, all ever known and unknown to humans, all that ever existed and will ever exist and many more.

उत्तरं यत्समुद्रस्य हिमाद्रेश्चैव दक्षिणम् ।

वर्षं तद् भारतं नाम भारती यत्र संततिः ॥

"The country (varṣam) that lies north of the ocean and south of the snowy mountains is called Bhāratam; there dwell the descendants of Bharata.

Chapter 5

The beginning of invasion in Akhand Bharat......

Once a wise sage who I was a disciple of told me that, dear son, always remember what you have today is the consequence of your deeds from the past you lived once and what you will be left with tomorrow will be the consequences of your deeds from the present you live now. So it got me thinking and then to an understanding that before we accept to have any kind of external disease in our body, we accept it in our mind that now we are the infected person and there is nothing that we can do to cure it. Before the body gets corrupted by external diseases the mind is. Any kind of diseases to take place in your body, you make yourself eat those corrupted and unhealthy food which later becomes the reason for that disease to take place into your body and that also happens because you are the one who accepted it in the mind to let it be consumed by you when you are hungry as people in your surrounding are doing the same. As you followed the unhealthy path now you are there alone to face the consequences of your habit to eat unhealthy food and your body weakening with every second that passes. From this we learn the lesson that for the physical body to be destroyed firstly the ethical and reasonable intellect or thinking of the mind should be corrupted to make it accept what is not good for the body and the mind in the long run.

Akhand Bharat was also invaded likewise. As we treated every guest with "Atithi Devo Bhava" meaning "a guest should be treated equally as a Dev should be treated", some of those Atithi were Danav in disguise of Dev like a wolf in the skin of sheep. They in the beginning came in small numbers as small merchants, wanderers, traders, scholars and believers of a religion, philosophy, ideology, way of life, etc., then learned all there was to learn from us about our knowledge, culture, functioning as a society, working as a gurukul and many other things that could have been the reason for our strength or the reason that could become a weakness of our destruction and can be used against us when the time comes. After learning about all that there was either they would become the lovely friend of this great bhumi maa Bharti due to the immense power this land holded to even win the heaven and heavenly gods on its own or the worst enemy who hated it all and wanted everything of it to be destroyed due to their attachment towards their insecurities; let them be the knowledge, people, mandirs, art, gurukuls, vyavastha, everything they hated it. Those enemies of the Sanatan dharma took either of the two paths for destruction of the cultural identity of the people of this land. One was to go back from where they came, so that they could inform their corrupt leaders about a country which is rich in culture and heritage, which has such immense wealth that even one simple trading ship was three times as bigger as their strongest army ship, which had mandirs full of precious treasures, whose people were immensely honest and obliged to their duties as citizen. This introduction of our motherland would make their leaders furious because of their jealousy and then they would be willing to invade us with alliances only formed to loot, kill, enslave and destroy everything and everyone of ours. The second was to stay here and pretend to be a friend a long time, so that they could become the part of our society due to which after a while they would have the access to strong social positions to deceive us and make unrighteous changes in our own functioning as a cultural society which would lead our innocent people to become a generation unable to have faith and make us disbelieve our own well functioning social structural invincible system and administration which was connected with mandirs in our own culture to finally destroy us internally. In the end both things happened in thousands of years then the Akhand Bharat became khandit which was one of many times united by many of the mighty and great kings let them be Chakravarti Shakuntala Putra Raja Bharat himself, Maryada Purushottam Sitapati Shri Raja Ramchandra, Kuntiputra DharmRaj Raja Udhisthir, Chakravarti Ujjain putra Samrat Vikramaditya and many other great sons and daughters of this janmabhumi and more important of all the avatar bhumi of Raj Rajeshwari Jagat Bhagwati Maa Amba, Param Pujya Paramatma Panchmukhi Sadashiv, Shri Vishnu Avatar Bramhan Shrestra Bhagwan Parshuram, Suryavanshi Maryada Purushottam Raja Shri Ramchandra, Yadukulshestra Dharamadhykhsha Dwarikadhisha Shri Krishnachanra.

'नमस्ते सदा वत्सले मातृभूमे त्वया हिन्दुभूमे सुखं वर्धितोहम्।

महामङ्गले पुण्यभूमे त्वदर्थे पतत्वेष कायो नमस्ते नमस्ते॥'

Namaste Sadā Vatsale Mātṛbhūme Tvayā Hindubhūme Sukhaṁ Vardhitohaṁ.

Mahāmaṅgale Puṇyabhūme Tvadarthe Patatveṣa Kāyo Namaste Namaste.

English Translation:

O love-loving mother-land, salutations to you always! This mother land has given us love and affection like our own children. I have grown up happily on this Hindu land. This land is a great and auspicious land. To protect this land, I offer my mortal body to the mother land and bow down to this land again and again.

Hindi Translation:

हे वात्सल्य-मयी मातृ-भूमि, तुम्हें सदा प्रणाम! इस मातृ-भूमि ने हमें अपने बच्चों की तरह स्नेह और ममता दी है। इस हिन्दू-भूमि पर सुखपूर्वक मैं बड़ा हुआ हूँ। यह भूमि महा मंगलमय और पुण्य-भूमि है। इस भूमि की रक्षा के लिए मैं यह नश्वर शरीर मातृ-भूमि को अर्पण करते हुए इस भूमि को बार बार प्रणाम करता हूँ।

CHAPTER 6

The invasion to destroy us, that has not stopped yet..

To destroy the Sanatan Dharma a series of invasions began more than two thousand years ago which still in the 21st century has not stopped yet. If you think it has stopped then you are just unaware of the truth in your surroundings and the source of your information as well as your education has cheated you all along. Let me help you through a small story, as a happy, smart, strong, free, financially well and healthy person is not always liked by many in society, who is also hated by some for what they have and haters of that person can't. Then the haters try different means to destroy the peace of the happy person and the reason for their strength, through different social, personal, intellectual or financial ways because it is the tendency of an uncontrolled, lazy, unambitious human mind to take every good thing others have for its own, through others destruction, as it can't work hard enough to earn it and be worthy of having it. The same is happening now everywhere in one way or the other, by one person or the other. The invasion of land from armies and swords has changed today into invasion of literature, entertainment, food and much more. Then at that time in the past the form of invasion was upfront aggressive in nature which was people of other countries and religion against our Bharat rashtra, our mandirs, our vishwavidyalaya and our Sanatan Sanskriti. It was people of other lands against our land in ancient times but now the definition of war and invasion has changed today into a somewhat passive-aggressive form of slow destruction like cancer. It was and always will be the ideology, the belief and the intellectual identity of an individual against the other at core for the reason of war and hate between people to ultimately stand against each other and be ruled an intruder through chaos among them. Weapons and armies were only an instrument of those intangible things to be tangibly achieved through aggressive mass destruction and killing in the past. Later on time changed, things changed, circumstances changed, people changed this lead to that aggressive form of invasion into passive form of slow destructive invasion. Through disbelief of our own people in our own culture and traditions, corruption in fundamental systematic structure of society, hatred of people of the same land against each other through lies, manipulated facts, linguistic differences and destruction of our strongest way of being a family into the society of confused,corrupted, self entitled, arrogant individuals; everything is the long term consequence of that passive form of invasion. Now if we have to stop this we will have to ultimately follow the path of dharma. One who wants to protect dharma should walk on the path of their swadharma to ultimately be worthy of being a righteous leader and a strong warrior for the descendants of Sanatan Dharma to follow them. Look at the history of our ancestors duties toward others, learn from what they did for the protection of our dharma as an individual representative of their own maryada, become the person who is the literal representation of their ancestors strength and many different things are there to be done for the suddhi of Bharat, first on the individual basis then on the institutional basis. When one wants to protect themself or others who they care for, they should start to strengthen themself in every way let it be physical, financial, intellectual or any other and in that process one should let go of all their impurities like iron when melted to latter become the strongest sword to be wielded for the protection of dharma. The strongest people to ever exist in the history of human civilization have always been defeated due to their weakness not because of their strength. To let go of all your impurities is the most important thing that is to be done, the reason for this action is to not let you be poisoned by the snake who you thought would serve you but a snake is always a snake which can never be trusted no matter what. Your unconquered insecurities, unnecessary attachments, uncontrolled desires and many other impurities might after a long period of time become the reason for you being unworthy to deserve what was always meant for you in the first place. The prince cannot become king after his father just because he is the rightful heir to the throne. To become the rightful king to deserve the throne, the prince will have to prove himself time to time to all the people of his kingdom, through his actions, his maturity, his nyay and his maryada

स्वराष्ट्रे न्यायवृत्तः स्याद् भृशदण्डश्च शत्रुषु ।

सुहृत्स्वजिह्मः स्निग्धेषु ब्राह्मणेषु क्षमान्वितः ॥ ३२ ॥

svarāṣṭre nyāyavṛttaḥ syād bhṛśadaṇḍaśca śatruṣu |

suhṛtsvajihmaḥ snigdheṣu brāhmaṇeṣu kṣamānvitaḥ || 32 ||

In his own kingdom he shall be of just behaviour, and on his enemies he shall inflict rigorous chastisement; with loved friends he shall be straightforward and towards Brāhmaṇas tolerant.—(32)

www.ingramcontent.com/pod-product-compliance
Lightning Source LLC
LaVergne TN
LVHW041643070526
838199LV00053B/3541